VEGETA

Cook Books from Amish Kitchens

Phyllis Pellman Good • Rachel Thomas Pellman

Good Books
Intercourse, PA 17534

VEGETABLES

Cook Books from Amish Kitchens

Gardens and their fruits are believed to be gifts. And they're treated as such. Vegetables are most often served gently

steamed and then covered with brown butter. But we haven't forgotten baked dried corn, potato filling, fried tomatoes, and home baked beans. All bring beauty and nutrition to any meal.

Cover art and design by Cheryl A. Benner.
Design and art in body by Craig N. Heisey; calligraphy by Gayle Smoker.
This special edition is an adaptation of *Vegetables: From Amish and Mennonite Kitchens, Pennsylvania Dutch Cookbooks,* and from *Cook Books by Good Books.* Copyright © 1982, 1991, 1996 by Good Books, Intercourse, PA 17534. ISBN: 1-56148-198-X. All rights reserved. Printed in the United States of America.

Contents

Baked Dried Corn 4
Scalloped Corn 4
Corn Fritters 5
Corn Pie 6
Home Baked Beans 7
Calico Beans 8
Baked Lima Beans 8
Potato Puffs 9
Crispy Topped Cheese Potatoes 10
Gourmet Cheese Potatoes 11
Libby's Spinach Potatoes 12
Potato Fritters 13
Mashed Potato Filling 14
Bread Filling 15
Sweet Potato Croquettes 16
Sweet Potato Pudding 17
Sweet Potato Apple Bake 18
Candied Sweet Potatoes 19
Baked Rice 20
Baked Carrots 20
Creamed Carrots 21
Green Beans with Tomatoes 22
Tomato Sauce 22
Fried Tomatoes 23
Peas and Knepp 24
Scalloped Celery and Cheese 25
Cauliflower Supreme 26
Broccoli, Cauliflower, or Asparagus with Cheese 27
Asparagus Loaf 28
Spinach with Dressing 28
Cheese-Eggplant Scallop 29
Fried Eggplant with Gravy 30
Harvard Beets 30
Beets in Orange Sauce 31
Onion Patties 32
Fried Onions 32

Baked Dried Corn

1 cup dried corn   Makes 8 servings
3 cups milk
½ tsp. salt
2 Tbsp. sugar
2 eggs, beaten
2 Tbsp. butter

1. Grind corn in food grinder or blender. Combine with milk and allow to stand ½ hour or more. Add salt, sugar, and eggs. Mix well.
2. Pour into a buttered 1 quart casserole dish. Dot with butter. Bake at 350° for 45-60 minutes.

Scalloped Corn

3 cups fresh,   Makes 6-8 servings
    frozen, or canned corn
3 eggs, beaten
1 cup milk
1½ tsp. salt
⅛ tsp. pepper
2 Tbsp. melted butter
buttered bread crumbs

1. Combine all ingredients except bread crumbs. Mix well. Pour into buttered 1-1½ quart casserole. Sprinkle with bread crumbs.
2. Bake, uncovered, at 350° for 1½ hours.

Variations:
   1. Add 1 Tbsp. flour or cornstarch.
   2. Add 1 Tbsp. minced onion.

Corn Fritters

   2 cups fresh, grated   Makes 12 fritters
      corn
   2 eggs, beaten
   ¾ cup flour
   ¾ tsp. salt
   ¼ tsp. pepper
   1 tsp. baking powder

1. Combine corn and eggs. Add flour which has been sifted with remaining ingredients.
2. Drop corn mixture from tablespoon into 1 inch of melted shortening. Fry until golden brown on both sides, turning once.

Corn Pie

Pastry for a 2- crust pie   Makes 8-10 servings
3 cups fresh corn
1½ cups raw potatoes, diced
2 or 3 hard-boiled eggs, diced
salt and pepper to taste
2 Tbsp. flour
milk

1. Line a casserole or deep pie pan with pastry.
2. Combine corn, potatoes, and eggs and pour into pastry lined container. Add salt and pepper. Sprinkle with flour. Add enough milk to cover the vegetables.
3. Cover with top pastry. Pinch edges together to seal.
4. Bake at 425° for 30-40 minutes, until crust is browned and milk is bubbly throughout.

Variation:
Add several slices of bacon cut into 1" pieces.

Home Baked Beans

1 lb. Great Northern navy beans
Makes 8-10 servings

1 tsp. salt
½ tsp. baking soda
1 small onion, minced
2 Tbsp. molasses
½ cup brown sugar
½ cup catsup
½ lb. bacon

1. Rinse and sort beans. Cover with 3 inches of water and allow to soak overnight. In the morning, add salt and soda and bring beans to a boil. Cook for ½ hour or until tender. More water should be added if beans become dry.
2. Pour into a 2 quart casserole and add remaining ingredients. Bacon should be fried until crisp and crumbled before adding. Bacon drippings may be added for additional flavor.
3. Bake at 325° for 1½-2 hours keeping covered with liquid.

Calico Beans

1 lb. hamburger   Makes 10 servings
¼ lb. bacon
1 medium onion, diced
1 large can pork 'n beans
1 can butter beans
1 can kidney beans
½ cup catsup
½ cup brown sugar
2 Tbsp. vinegar
½ tsp. salt

1. Brown hamburger, bacon, and onion in skillet. Combine meat and all beans. Pour into a greased casserole.
2. Combine catsup, brown sugar, vinegar, and salt. Pour over meat and beans.
3. Bake at 350° for 1 hour.

Baked Lima Beans

1 quart lima beans   Makes 4-6 servings
1 Tbsp. cornstarch
¼ cup water
½ lb. bacon
1 Tbsp. prepared mustard

3 Tbsp. brown sugar
2 Tbsp. King Syrup molasses

1. Boil beans until soft. Drain off excess water. Combine cornstarch and water and add to beans. Cook till thickened.
2. Fry bacon until crisp. Drain. Crumble and add to beans.
3. Add remaining ingredients. Pour into baking dish. Bake at 350° for 30 minutes.

Potato Puffs

1 cup mashed potatoes   Makes 12 puffs
2 eggs, beaten
¼ tsp. salt
⅓ cup flour
1 tsp. baking powder
shortening

1. Combine all ingredients except shortening and mix well. Deep fry until golden brown in hot shortening using 1 large tsp. of potato mixture for each puff.

Crispy Topped Cheese Potatoes

5 Tbsp. melted butter   Makes 4 servings
4 medium potatoes, cooked until
    almost soft
1 cup cornflakes, finely crushed
½ tsp. paprika
1 tsp. salt
1 cup shredded cheese

1. Pour 2 Tbsp. melted butter into shallow baking pan. Cut potatoes into ½" slices and place close together in pan. Brush tops with remaining butter.
2. Combine cornflakes, paprika, salt, and cheese. Sprinkle over potatoes.
3. Bake at 350° for 25 minutes.

Variations:
    1. Add a sprinkle of red pepper to cornflake mixture.
    2. Leave skins on potatoes.

Gourmet Cheese Potatoes

6 medium potatoes   Makes 6 servings
2 cups shredded cheddar cheese
¼ cup butter
1½ cups sour cream or milk
⅓ cup onion, chopped
1 tsp. salt
¼ tsp. pepper
2 Tbsp. butter
paprika

1. Cook potatoes in skins. Shred coarsely.
2. In saucepan over low heat combine cheese and butter. Stir until melted. Remove from heat and add sour cream, onion, salt, and pepper. Fold sauce into potatoes.
3. Pour into greased casserole. Dot with butter. Sprinkle with paprika.
4. Bake at 350° for 30 minutes or until bubbly throughout.

"We like the sour cream and cheese flavors."

Libby's Spinach Potatoes

1 10 oz. pkg. frozen   Makes 6 servings
   spinach
6-8 large potatoes, cooked and mashed
¾ cup sour cream
2 tsp. salt
1 tsp. sugar
¼ tsp. pepper
2 tsp. chopped chives
¼ tsp. dill weed
4 Tbsp. butter or margarine melted
1 cup grated cheese

1. Thaw and drain spinach.
2. Combine all ingredients except cheese.
Mix well. Place in greased casserole and
top with cheese.
3. Bake at 400° for 20 minutes.

"This is good, nutritious, and uses
ingredients I'm likely to have on hand."

Potato Fritters

4 cups mashed potatoes   Makes about 10 fritters

2 eggs, well beaten

2 Tbsp. parsley, finely chopped

½ onion, finely chopped

¼ cup pimento, minced

2 tsp. baking powder

flour

1. Combine all ingredients and mix well. Flour may be added if needed so potatoes can be shaped. Fritters may be fried like pancakes in a skillet or dropped by spoonfuls into hot fat. If enough flour is added potatoes can be formed into balls and rolled in crushed cornflakes before deep frying.

"An interesting way to use leftover mashed potatoes."

Mashed Potato Filling

½ cup butter　　　　　Makes 10 servings
½ cup celery, chopped
2 Tbsp. onion, chopped
4 cups soft bread cubes
1 pinch saffron
½ cup boiling water
3 eggs, beaten
2 cups milk
1½ tsp. salt
2 cups mashed potatoes

1. Melt butter. Add celery and onion. Cook until tender. Pour over bread cubes and mix well.
2. Combine saffron and boiling water. Add to bread and mix well. Add remaining ingredients to bread, mixing well after each addition. Finished product should be very moist. Add more milk if necessary.
3. Turn into 2 well greased casserole dishes. Bake at 350° for 45 minutes.

Bread Filling

4 eggs　　　　　　　　Makes 6 servings
2 cups milk
2 quarts soft bread cubes
4 Tbsp. melted butter
1 Tbsp. parsley, chopped
1 tsp. onion, minced
1 tsp. salt
1 tsp. sage or poultry seasoning

1. Beat eggs. Add milk. Pour over bread cubes.
2. Combine butter and seasonings. Add to bread cubes and mix well.
3. Filling can be baked in a casserole dish at 350° for 45 minutes or may be used as stuffing for fowl.

"I use regular bread and break it into small pieces instead of buying bread cubes."

15

Sweet Potato Croquettes

Sweet potatoes
Bread crumbs
Margarine

1. Wash potatoes thoroughly. Cook until tender. Peel potatoes while hot. Mash them immediately with electric mixer. Beat until smooth. Potato fibers will cling to beaters.
2. Chill mashed potatoes for several hours in refrigerator. Shape potatoes into uniform croquettes approximately 3"x1¼". Roll in bread crumbs.
3. Fry croquettes in margarine, turning so all sides brown. Serve immediately. Croquettes may be frozen at this point and reheated in an oven at 325° for 20 minutes.

Variation:
Add 3 Tbsp. brown sugar per 2 cups mashed sweet potatoes.

Sweet Potato Pudding

2 cups mashed
   sweet potatoes
3 Tbsp. sugar
2 eggs, well beaten
2 Tbsp. melted butter
1 tsp. salt
1 cup milk
½ cup miniature marshmallows or
   marshmallow creme

Makes 4-6 servings

1. Combine all ingredients except marshmallows. Blend well.
2. Pour into buttered casserole. Top with marshmallows.
3. Bake at 350° for 45 minutes.

You may wait to add marshmallows until the last 20 minutes of baking time. They will then be golden brown to serve.

"This is one vegetable our whole family enjoys!"

17

Sweet Potato Apple Bake

6 medium sweet   Makes 6-8 servings
  potatoes
2 or 3 apples
¼ cup margarine
⅓ cup brown sugar
1 Tbsp. flour
1 tsp. salt
2 Tbsp. orange juice

1. Cook sweet potatoes until soft. Peel and cut in half lengthwise.
2. Peel and slice apples.
3. Combine remaining ingredients.
4. Layer ingredients in casserole making first a layer of potatoes, then apples, then half of the orange juice mixture. Repeat, topping with remaining orange juice mixture.
5. Bake at 350° for 1 hour.

"The apples really compliment the sweet potatoes."

Candied Sweet Potatoes

6 medium sweet potatoes   Makes 6 servings
salt
paprika
¾ cup brown sugar
½ tsp. grated lemon rind
1½ Tbsp. lemon juice
2 Tbsp. butter

1. Cook potatoes until soft. Peel and cut lengthwise in ½ inch slices. Place in shallow, greased baking dish. Sprinkle with salt and paprika.
2. Mix sugar, lemon rind, and lemon juice. Drizzle over potatoes.
3. Dot with butter.
4. Bake, uncovered, at 375° for 20 minutes. Baste several times during baking.

"This is an easy make-ahead dish. We used to cook the sweet potatoes Saturday night; then have them sliced and candied for Sunday lunch."

Baked Rice

2 Tbsp. butter   Makes 4 servings
1 medium onion, chopped
1¼ cup rich beef broth
⅔ cup water
1 cup uncooked, long grain rice
slivered almonds

1. Sauté onion in butter. Add broth and water. Bring to a boil.
2. Place rice in a buttered casserole. Pour hot broth mixture over rice. Cover and bake at 350° for 40-45 minutes. Sprinkle with almonds.

Baked Carrots

2½ cups cooked,   Makes 6-8 servings
    mashed carrots
1 Tbsp. onion, minced
3 eggs, well beaten
2 cups rich milk
3 Tbsp. melted butter
½ cup bread crumbs
salt and pepper to taste

1. Combine all ingredients. Pour into greased casserole.
2. Bake, uncovered, at 375° for 1 hour.

Creamed Carrots

4 cups carrots, sliced   Makes 8 servings
salt and pepper to taste
3 Tbsp. butter
1 Tbsp. onion, chopped
3 Tbsp. flour
1½ cup milk
1 cup grated cheese

1. Cook carrots. Season with salt and pepper; then place in greased casserole dish.
2. Melt butter. Add onion and cook until tender. Add flour and stir until smooth. Gradually add milk, stirring constantly, and cook until thickened. Add cheese and stir until melted.
3. Pour sauce over carrots and stir gently. Bake at 350° for 30-35 minutes.

    This dish is also very good with green beans.

Green Beans with Tomatoes

1 quart cooked   Makes 6-8 servings
  green beans
4 Tbsp. butter
¼ cup onion, chopped
¼ cup green pepper, diced
1 cup canned tomatoes
1 tsp. flour
1 tsp. salt
⅛ tsp. pepper

1. Melt butter. Sauté green beans, onion, and green pepper until lightly browned.
2. Mix flour, salt, and pepper with tomatoes. Add to green bean mixture and cook slowly for 6-8 minutes.

Tomato Sauce

2 Tbsp. butter   Makes 6 servings
3 Tbsp. flour
4 Tbsp. brown sugar
1 quart canned tomatoes

1. Melt butter in heavy skillet. Add flour and stir until flour browns and mixture

becomes crumbly.
2. Add brown sugar and tomatoes with juice. Stir until mixture thickens. This may be served alone or over toast. It's a good compliment to a fish dinner.

Fried Tomatoes

3 firm, almost   Makes 6-8 servings
    ripe tomatoes
1 egg, beaten
2 Tbsp. milk
1 cup cracker crumbs
¼ cup shortening
salt and pepper to taste

1. Slice tomatoes into ¾ inch slices.
2. Combine egg and milk. Dip each tomato slice in egg mixture and then into cracker crumbs.
3. Melt shortening and fry coated tomato slices. Brown on both sides, turning once. Season with salt and pepper.

Peas and Knepp

1½ cups flour   Makes 10-12 servings
2 tsp. baking powder
¾ tsp. salt
3 Tbsp. shortening
¾ cup milk
6 cups fresh peas
butter

1. Combine flour, baking powder, and salt. Cut in shortening. Blend in milk.
2. Place peas in large kettle and add enough water to cover peas. Cook about 10 minutes.
3. Drop knepp dough by spoonfuls on top of boiling peas. Cook slowly for 10 minutes, uncovered. Cover with dome lid and cook 10 minutes longer. Serve drizzled with browned butter.

Knepp can be made with any vegetable in season.

Scalloped Celery and Cheese

3 cups celery, diced   Makes 6 servings
1 Tbsp. butter
3 Tbsp. flour
1½ cups milk
½ cup celery liquid
¾ tsp. salt
dash of pepper
1 cup grated cheese
1 cup buttered crumbs

1. Cook celery in water until tender. Drain, reserving ½ cup of liquid.
2. Melt butter. Add flour and stir until smooth. Gradually add milk and celery liquid. Cook, stirring constantly until thickened. Add salt, pepper, and cheese. Stir until cheese melts.
3. In greased casserole place a layer of celery, then cheese sauce, then buttered crumbs. Repeat, ending with crumbs.
4. Bake at 350° for 30-40 minutes.

Cauliflower Supreme

1 head cauliflower   Makes 6-8 servings
salt to taste
2 cups tomatoes
2 Tbsp. flour
2 Tbsp. water
3 Tbsp. sugar
cheese slices

1. Break cauliflower head into pieces and cook with salt until tender. Drain well and place in greased casserole dish.
2. Put tomatoes in saucepan and bring to a boil. Make a paste of flour and water and add to tomatoes. Cook until thickened. Add sugar. Pour sauce over cauliflower. Top with slices of cheese.
3. Bake until cheese is bubbly and browned, about 30-35 minutes at 375°.

"This is a simple dish to prepare. We think it's very good!"

Broccoli, Cauliflower, or Asparagus with Cheese

1 head broccoli or   Makes 6-8 servings
  cauliflower or 1 bunch of asparagus
cheese sauce

1. Cut vegetable into pieces. Cook until soft.
Drain. Serve with cheese sauce.

Cheese Sauce
    4 Tbsp. butter
    4 Tbsp. flour
    1 tsp. salt
    2 cups milk
    ½ cup cheese

1. Melt butter. Stir in flour and salt.
2. Gradually add milk, stirring constantly.
Cook until smooth and thickened.
3. Add cheese and stir until melted. Pour
sauce over vegetable.

Variation:
    Sprinkle buttered bread crumbs over
cheese sauce.

Asparagus Loaf

1 quart cooked asparagus
1 quart bread cubes
4 eggs
2 cups milk
2 Tbsp. melted butter
1 tsp. salt

Makes 8-10 servings

1. Combine all ingredients. Turn into greased loaf pan or casserole dish.
2. Bake at 350° for 45-60 minutes.

Spinach with Dressing

10-12 oz. frozen spinach
1 Tbsp. mayonnaise
1 tsp. mustard
½ tsp. sugar
¼ tsp. vinegar

Makes 4 servings

1. Cook spinach. Drain.
2. Combine all other ingredients. Pour over hot spinach. Serve immediately.

Cheese-Eggplant Scallop

1 eggplant   Makes 6 servings
¼ lb. margarine
½ lb. bread cubes
2 eggs, beaten
¼ lb. grated cheese
salt and pepper to taste

1. Peel eggplant. Cut into chunks and cook in a small amount of water until tender. Drain. Mash lightly with potato masher.
2. Melt margarine. Add margarine to bread cubes. Divide bread cubes in half. To one half add eggplant, eggs, half of cheese, and salt and pepper.
3. Place half of remaining bread cubes in bottom of greased 1 quart casserole. Add eggplant mixture. Top with remaining bread cubes and sprinkle with remaining cheese.
4. Bake at 350° for 30 minutes.

Fried Eggplant with Gravy

1 large eggplant   Makes 4-6 servings
flour
shortening
brown sugar
milk
salt

1. Peel eggplant and slice in 3/4" slices. Dip each slice in flour to coat both sides. Sauté in small amount of shortening until browned.
2. Sprinkle each slice with brown sugar.
3. Add milk enough to cover the browned slices. Reduce heat and simmer till milk is somewhat thickened and eggplant is soft. Salt to taste.

Harvard Beets

1/3 cup sugar   Makes 6 servings
1 Tbsp. cornstarch
1 tsp. salt
1/4 cup vinegar
1/4 cup water

3 cups cooked beets, sliced or diced
2 Tbsp. butter

1. Combine sugar, cornstarch, and salt. Add vinegar and water. Stir until smooth. Bring mixture to a boil and cook 5 minutes.
2. Add beets to hot mixture and allow to stand for 30 minutes.
3. Just before serving bring to a boil and add butter.

Beets in Orange Sauce

1 lb. cooked sliced beets   Makes 4 servings
1½ tsp. cornstarch
½ tsp. salt
3 Tbsp. firmly packed brown sugar
½ cup orange juice
1 Tbsp. butter

1. Thoroughly drain beets.
2. In saucepan combine cornstarch, salt, and brown sugar. Gradually add orange juice. Add butter. Cook stirring constantly until thickened and clear.
3. Add beets. Heat thoroughly.

Onion Patties

¾ cup flour   Makes 6-8 patties
2 tsp. baking powder
1 Tbsp. sugar
½ tsp. salt
1 Tbsp. corn meal
¾ cup milk
2 ½ cups onion, finely chopped
shortening

1. Combine dry ingredients. Add milk and mix well.
2. Stir in onions. Drop batter in small mounds into hot shortening. Fry until golden brown on both sides, turning once.

Fried Onions

Slice onions in butter in frying pan and sauté until slightly browned and tender. Add a little salt and vinegar and serve on top of potatoes boiled in their jackets.